EMBRACE

Are You Living? Or Are You Existing?

Chaplain CL Connor

INTRODUCTION
WHO ARE YOU?

W ho Are You?" Who do you think you are? What do people say you are? We lives in a time where it is so easy and common to allow others to dictate our identity, our actions, and our direction in life. It is as if they have the power to tell us when to go and when to stop in our life's journey. Does this sound like you? Can you look in the mirror and honestly say "I am in control: of my life, my actions, MY IDENTITY," or is the conversation more along the lines of, "I *think* I know who I am, where I'm going, what I want to accomplish, but my friends, my family, my peers say otherwise.

It is quite common to identify more with the second question when you take a moment to retrace some of the steps you have taken in life; when you truly learn to look at yourself and how your life has progressed from childhood to adulthood. Are you living your dream? Are you even working towards *your* dream? I put an emphasis on *your* because you would be surprised how many people, unknowingly, have been reduced to and settled for a goal/dream that really is not theirs, but one that was encouraged by someone else; a friend, a family member, a boss, etc. We end up trying to be what someone pushed and dictated to us instead of being our unique design by God.

There is the saying "the eyes are the window of the world." Have you ever taken a long look at yourself in the mirror; looking past the surface for beautification, but a deep, long look into the inner you? Do you like what you see? Do you want to look within. We are so engulfed in our outer, appearance that we fail to take that true look within. We do not want to see the pain, the emotion, the secrets that dwell inside our very being; but would much rather be content with being beautiful on the outside and *convince* ourselves that same beauty lives within us. We end up becoming completely lost and unfamiliar of whom we truly are and content with who others tell us we ought to be.

This book is to help you and others find your *true* self so that you can grow and start living your *true* life. You have to believe in you and whatever higher power you believe in has for you. It's time to live! Are you really living or are you existing?

CHAPTER 1

WHAT IS EXISTING?

Are we living or existing? Existing is only a temporary season; whether it is a dream, some idea, or some definition of where we should be or go, existing is, merely, an impermanent following. Has your life gotten to be routine? Every day it's getting up, going to work/school, coming home, paying the bills, tending to the children doing the laundry, then going to bed only to wake up and repeat the same cycle all over again? *That* is existing! Going through life experiencing the same series of events day in and day out with nothing, changing; nothing giving your life a spark of spontaneity and mystery. With such a routine when do you laugh? Do you wake up with the excitement of taking on a new day and its many adventures? Do you even have the time to just stop and say, "Thank you, God, for this day that you have given me?" When you are just going through the motions of existing, you are showing signs of contentment; which, in some cases, leads to a yearning for something more out of life.

We are Americans: we want more. We want larger, bigger, better because society has dictated and developed the ideology that more is better. More brings status. More is SUCCESS. Contrary to that premise, more is not always better and this way of thinking tends to lead to the inability to appreciate what you may already have accomplished. If we can grow and *be* the person we really want to be, we can enjoy, we can have bank accounts, we can travel, smile, appreciate and celebrate life. That is how you live. That is what *living* is.

Existing is just being on this earth until the day you die. Your life starts to dwindle into a space lacking breath taking moments and unforgettable memories. Is that what you want? Is that what you are looking for? That was not the choice I made for my life and I do not think most of you want that either. Unfortunately, a lot of people lie to themselves; saying that they are happy with an uneventful lifestyles. This acceptance of the mundane to stem from not only a level of comfort, but also fear of change. So they end up believing this self told lie that they are truly happy and see nothing wrong with routine: with the repetitive cycle that have created for their lives.

They tell others this same lie; to paint the false image of happiness that they claim to have in the efforts of receiving the approval of their peers. They end up looking for self-fulfillment and guidance in all the wrong places. They search for male companionship father figures, mother figures, sisters, brothers, just someone to tell them how they should live, but when advice is given that brings change to the life *routine* they have already devoted themselves to, do they really hear it? No! That is because they are not looking for guidance, they are looking for approval. They are looking for someone to agree with how they are living and not critiques them.

These are people you do not want to be around. They turn into the closed-minded "Can't nobody tell me how to live my life" type of people whenever they are offered any type of advice that could add a little spice to their unchanging lifestyle. They hit you with the "I'm grown: attack followed by the "I pay my own bills and live my life argument," but fail to see that they aren't really *living* at all, but only existing in the robot-like reality of wake up, work, eat, sleep, repeat. Now be honest; did that just describe you? Tell the truth. You can't live a *real* life without keeping *real* with yourself first.

When you live, you leave memories and people that enjoy being around you. People say, "Wow, they are always smiling. They really are enjoying life! They don't have the huge house or the most expensive car or the high paying job, but they're truly happy and they are always going somewhere." Most importantly, when you live, you live for YOU! We tend to get in the habit of worrying about what other people say about our lifestyle. It is amazing how people who don't pay ANY of our bills have gained so much influence in some of the decisions we make in our lives. We worry about what they're going to do, how they think, what they want, how they feel about a life that isn't even theirs. The false need for the approval of others has resulted in so many people giving the control of their own happiness to other people.

We also relinquish the power to control our own happiness by comparing our lives and circumstances to others. You see a co-worker, or friend, or family member bragging and flaunting their new outfit, diamonds, and brand new sport car and the attention they're getting from it all and start to lost the appreciation for the things you have and start to develop the desire for what they have. You want the nice things and the attention. You want that dream life, but ask yourself, "Do I really want that? Is that truly my heart's desire? Or am I trying to replicate *their* dream; live *their* lifestyles?"

Let's look at how we need to go about living. There are changes we have to make. We have to be truthful with ourselves. Truth is one of the hardest things to grasp and accept. It's not easy to say, "I can't afford this or that right now but I'm going to enjoy what I do have now," to someone. Why is it so hard to say the words, "I don't have" to someone? Have you ever wondered that? Maybe we need to ask ourselves that question more often. Perhaps it comes with a feeling of lack. Feeling like you just don't have enough to do what you want; to have what you want; to go where you want. Perhaps it opens up the door to another feeling rooted in the questions; the feeling of not doing enough; not *being* enough to get all you want out of life. Maybe it's fear; the fear of someone's disapproval; the fear of being looked down upon; the fear of judgment by your peers or family.

More often than not, it takes a while to break these self-inflicted shackles we put on our mind. If you're a mother, your're raising children; if you're a father, you're raising children. If you're a husband, you're taking care of a wife; sometimes the wife is taking care of the husband; but if you're single, you may feel alone at times, you feel that you're empty; you feel, that you didn't make the cut. You may ask yourself, "Why didn't anyone want to marry me? Why can't I be loved? Why am I not important?" These are examples of the mental shackles we put on ourselves.

The negative thoughts you place on yourself and truly believe in have a way of becoming instilled. You become that person. You allow yourself to wallow in your self-pity. You made that choice. We all have choices in life. Maybe God is working on you to do something better. Maybe there is something better coming into your life. Perhaps that is why you are single. Maybe you are built for something more in life. Don't waste your time and energy wondering why, how, where, and when. Focus on now and developing the best version of yourself for yourself.

CHAPTER 2

PROJECT

What is our project? Our project is ourselves. We think our project is fixing our families, our children, our husband, our boyfriend and our parents. The project is ourselves. Look at yourself and start reconstructing.

The things you don't like—change them. You have a choice. The things you want to do—do them. You have a choice. We let things like "I don't have the money," and "I can't" control us. No such vocabulary should be used if you want to live life and not just exist in life. Only positive should be spoken.

People, you are looking at others that have reached their goals in life and still climbing because they didn't believe in the word can't, and they achieve the things they achieve because "don't" and "can't" are not in their vocabularies. You can achieve it, if you believe it. Maybe not on my time, but everybody opens up their own gift in their own season. Now you may have to go around a few times until you truly start believing in yourself. You may need to change your job and go back to school; maybe you have to change your direction to reach your goals one at a time.

We have to stop shopping every time we get upset, buying new pairs of shoes, clothes, shirts, dresses, whatever. Stop buying. Start banking if you want a house. Start checking out your credit report; three credit reports are free every year. Call them. Get them. Start working on them. Dissect them one at a time, and eventually you will reach your goal. Every time you want to go and purchase your lunch think about your plans and bring your lunch; save your money. Stop always complaining that you don't have, but you look at your budget and you know you are spending more than you have. Move somewhere that may be in your budget or whatever you need to do to reach your goals in the end.

Start saving! Start investing! Start thinking with wisdom. Use discernment. We all have it; we just don't use it. Our project is ourselves. Your project is from the top of your head to the bottom of your toes. Take one step, and start moving forward and stop going backward. Stop looking backward. The past is the past. It's our history of who we are; it's not who we have to be. What your parents may have done, or what your father may have been, or how you might have been raised, or what you might have seen that you shouldn't have seen, that is your past.

It doesn't have to be your future. We have to look forward to our future; that's why we have to use this project. "Our project is redeveloping, building, constructing" a new you just like you're building a new building. Step by step, you have to lay the groundwork. You have to come up with the plans, you have to get the permit, you have to get the license, you have to start structuring the framework, and then you start building a building; that's the same thing we do for ourselves.

Make a foundation. Have a game plan. Let that plan go to where you want it to be. Let that plan make your design goals. Every year, write a goal list; include three things, and accomplish those three things—you will eventually reach those goals. I am thankful that I have reached my goals, and I am still climbing, and I believe "All things are possible through God, who has strengthening me." That is my belief—it doesn't have to be yours, but it is my belief. My thing is this: you are a project, and the only project is you. You cannot love anyone else until you love yourself.

CHAPTER 3
WHY SHOULD YOU LOVE?

Love is a thing that is one of the most common words used in the Bible. Love was dictated to us. Some people think love is just Valentine's Day—getting a gift, giving a present. "That's how you love me. Giving me money—that's how you love me." That's why they are still empty. That's why they are still hurting. That's why the pain is still in them—because they think materialistic things are what make love.

Some people think love is having sex. You are laying there screwing Johnny, Paul, Tom, Susan, Mary, or Jane. You think that is love because you had a sexual intercourse. That's lust. Fornication. Call it what it is. Horny. Whatever you want to see it as. You're just having a good time, and you're just splurging your body and using it as a weapon to get something. Alright? Don't confuse that with love.

Love is someone who is going to love you if you don't have two legs. Love is someone who will love you if you become blind. Love is someone who is going to stand by you if you don't have a job. Love is someone who will stand by you and walk with you through the good times and the bad. Love is someone that will not walk away the minute things get tough. Love is something that doesn't change. It's called unconditional love.

Don't fool yourself and think that Johnny is buying you some new earrings, getting your hair done, paying for your pedicure and manicure and you paying him back by sexing him up; that is purely fornication, and you're being used. U-s-e-d. The word is "used." You're being used, and he's being used. You're using him for the money, and he's using you for the body. Ladies you need to wake up and smell the coffee. "That is not love." He pays your rent—that is not love because he has a key to the house. Love is unconditional. You're not looking for something back in return.

Stop reading those books and watching those reality shows and thinking, "Well, it's love." Susie sleeps with Billy; Billy sleeps with Pauline. Pauline sleeps with Jane. Today, with this generation of sex and love, it's nothing but fornication and lust; that's why we have many issues with sexually transmitted diseases in our times. Close your legs, and start using your brain.

CHAPTER 4

DICTATION

Dictation is something that we say; we take notes. We type, we listen, we use recordings, we do things, but dictation of a person is when you're allowing someone to dictate your life; man or woman. Someone to tell you what direction to go. You have your husband saying, "No, you don't need to go to work. You stay at home and take care of the kids." And then when he divorces you, you don't have any skills because you're allowing your life to be dictated to. Men, it's when your woman says, "Honey, let me pay all the bills," and then when you look at your bank account, it's empty, and she's gone because you allowed her to dictate your life.

A relationship is not dictation. No one is the dictator. A relationship is two combined people talking over a plan to come together as one. It is not a dictatorship. We are American citizens. We do not rule over another person. Your opinion really doesn't matter on this right now, you either agree with me or disagree with me. We come to agree he isn't going to know anything I have. She isn't going to know anything I have. Why don't you just stay single and you each stay in your own corner? You create children, and you realize the truth—that you both were underhanded, sneaky and running around doing all those things, and now you have innocent children involved in this and now you are going your separate ways and who is suffering? God covers the little children. You think he's in love with you and next thing you are saying, "I want a baby" and "I love him today," but two years from now, you can't *stand* him or you hate him." They say it's a thin line between love and hate. Oh yeah, it's a thin line between love and hate.

Stop bringing children into your mess. You don't even know who you are. Learn who you are before you decide to bring children into your mess, and stop bringing men around your children that you know you are not going to stay with. Your children don't need to meet every Jonas, Theodore, Paul, or Gary or whoever, and they definitely don't need to meet every Susan, Mary, Kelly, or Kate. Stop bringing all these people around your children. Your children are so confused; they have so many aunts, uncles, mamas, and daddies. They don't even know which way they are going.

They are growing up into another dysfunctional generation because of what we brought into it. "I don't have time to help my child study, but I have time to go have sex with Mary or Paul at three o'clock in the morning."

This is ridiculous. Stop bringing people around your children, letting people stay in your house, letting people see your surroundings. You ask why your children don't respect you when they get older; well, you didn't respect them. To get respect, you have to give respect, and you haven't gained it because of the actions you are taking.

Stop crying about the same old things if you're going to do the same thing. I mean, really, honestly, if he doesn't have his own place, why is he sleeping at your house? You know. Why is he sleeping there with your children? Yet, you wonder why your children's daddy does not pay child support. It's because you have a man laying up in your home not doing anything. That's wrong, and I don't agree with it. The fact is that your children don't know who's their daddy is anymore and then you say. "Oh, I broke up with Johnny, and now Paul is coming over. This is your uncle Paul." Then "Uncle

Paul" is in the bed with Mommy. Paul is walking around in his underwear. What kind of influence is that on your children?

Let me repeat myself, wake up and smell the coffee. Cut it out and understand sex is not all that! You only have eighteen to twenty-three years to raise your children. Give your child that time. You made the decision to open your legs to have them, and then you are angry because you have to raise them alone. "My child is failing in school. The teacher doesn't like my child." Bull!

You aren't studying with your child. When are you spending quality time with your child? It's not the teachers fault that your children don't have discipline because all the anger is coming out in the classroom. They can't stay at home because you curse them out and smack them, Yet, you are go to church and praise the Lord. This is your example of serving your higher power.

Children will come back and give back the love you gave. You give them nothing, and they will give you nothing back. They will grow up following the same patterns and the same hurts. It's a family generational curse is over and over again. These men don't love your children. They don't even love you and you know that, but they are helping you pay the bills sometimes, but probably causing your bills to be higher from living in your house.

Well, if you stop spending and live within your means, you don't need a man to pay the bills. You don't need a woman to pay the bills. You don't need to settle because you feel your worth is nothing. Someone told you in your life that you are worth nothing. Yes, your mother and father might have been drug addicts or sex addicts or whatever addicts they were, but you don't have to be that way. You have a choice.

Just because you were pregnant at sixteen, you don't have to be punished the rest of your life. You can still build a life. Go to school; education is a way out the door. Stop saying you can't learn; go get your GED if you don't have it. Stop complaining and saying you can't. The thing is you are just being plain lazy and you won't.

That's the truth. It's time to keep moving and to stop using the word "can't." It is not a word to live by. The correct thing to say "I can." Thank you, Obama, "I can." He said, "I can," and I believe I can. We need to start believing that we can accomplish the things that are designed for us to do. Stop telling your child we can't do that, but you can't give your child (ren) that we can't get them new clothes for school and school uniforms, but you will pay $100 for pair of sneakers that they will not be able to wear in 6 months

The child can wear a less expensive sneaker. They don't pay any bills, and if you give them everything at an early age, how do they learn to earn things for themselves? Your child is getting grades of Ds and Fs, but you reward them with the latest video cell phone or expensive clothes—really? Wake up and smell the coffee! Start saving your money; invest in your children's future education, tutoring, music lessons, activities, and things that will give them value in life. Women, wake up.

When children's get in high school and they earn their grades and get averages like 3.5 or 4.0, then yes, you want to buy them something special, every now and then. You are on the budget or striding for a vacation with your family. You can't purchasing Jimmy Choo shoes, when you can't afford to pay your rent or mortgage. This is ridiculous. Spending money on a manicure and pedicure every week—you are not Oprah. Their nails are natural, but you are using fake nails and can't pay the electric bill on time.

Most people with money don't have fake nails on. I don't know, but today is a new day and you have to decide what is truly important to you. Yes, you can get a manicure and pedicure, if your bills and your children are taken care of and it not causing a hardship. You can't pay your bills then you need to purchase you a small bottle of polish and do it yourself. You might not agree with me, but it's real.

Life is a mystery. You never know who might walk in your front door. Sometimes people say, "I can't find that special someone to love me; appreciate me; complete me; to make me happy." It's because you're looking! Take care of yourself and maybe as you focus on working on *you* someone will come along who sweeps you off your feet. If you aren't truly happy with yourself and who you have grown to be, meeting a nice man or woman doesn't even matter because you still won't be happy. Why? Because how can you work on building a happy relationship with someone who isn't happy, or when you, yourself aren't happy. So now you're in a position where you're trying to work on yourself and a relationship instead of being able to put all of your energy into just one. And through doing that, how can anyone fine happiness?

CHAPTER 5
FIND YOUR TRUE SELF

Men think they know what you want.

I love me some Steve Harvey, but how are you going to let a man tell you how to "Act Like a Lady, Think Like A Man" I mean, the book was great and I truly enjoyed it and I give him praise on it, but I believe a woman needs to be taught by a woman.

You need to look at yourself and see that you are a woman; Some women have embraced the male role so much that when a man, who is interested, does come along they come off with a more masculine demeanor than that of a woman. You have to be aware of that, ladies. Yes, situations can place you in a role of being mother and a father, but you do not have to exhibit that masculine behavior because of it.

In a season of my life the role of mother and father was placed upon me after divorce. However, during that season I have never desired to think like a man. I loved who God designed me to be; a unique, strong woman and that love gave me the drive to carry out my duties of going to work, paying the bills, and continuing my education to higher levels so that I could provide the best life for my children that I could. I didn't need a man to tell me how to be a woman; my mother and other positive influential women whom where in my life taught me and instilled in me the characteristics that allowed me to grow into a woman of virtue and dignity. From the way that I dressed to the way I carried myself in the eyes of others. I found and nurtured my confidence and established my self worth to such a high degree, that I didn't want to be anything or anyone else. We all have our own truth of who we think we are in this life. Look in the mirror. Look at the person staring back at you and tell that person your own truth of who you are. Say it, claim it, and live it! Don't exist for anyone but you!

You want a husband, but you're not letting any suitors be a man for you. You don't let them open doors, pay for dinner on dates, or any other gesture and you hinder a man's attempts of being a gentleman to you because you're so used to doing for yourself and playing both roles that you forget how to just be a woman. Well, this has potential to lead to you never being able to find or keep a man, because, hey, in their mind, "What does she need a man for? She is one!"

A common issue some women face is that they, sometimes unknowingly, try and dictate to a man *how* to be a man. I have been asked countless times, "Chaplain CL How can I meet a man who could be a potential husband? What kind of a woman are men looking to marry?" Well, my personal opinion is a man wants a positive, uplifting woman. One who he can rely on and grow with. Also, a man is looking for a woman who shows some class and self-respect about herself. A woman doesn't have to open her legs to every Paul, Peter and Johnny. Respect yourself, ladies, and a man will respect you! I'm not trying to sound preachy, but as the saying goes, :Don't go looking for a man; let the man find you." The Bible tells us in Proverb 18:22, "He who finds a good thing." So be patient ladies, he's coming!

Some men will take what you give to him. If you have sex with him immediately, he is thinking, "Why would I marry you? Why should I marry you?" He has everything. He has your house key, he has your bed, and he's telling you what to do, which way to go. Why would he marry you? He has no respect for you because you have no respect for yourself.

He's telling you what to do and which way to go. You need to be effeminate, attractive, to smell good, and to do something with that hair. All these colored wigs and weaves do not make you attractive; you attract the type of man by the way you carry yourself.

Just because it is a style, you don't have to wear it; everything is not for everyone. You are not a movie star or out on a stage. Why are you out in the street looking like you're some Nicki Minaj? You are not getting paid her money. Stop putting every red, purple, blue, or yellow wig on your head and think you look cute. You look like you're going on Forty-Second Street to be a hooker. "No man wants to talk to you, only the one who wants to tap that booty." Booty shorts up your butt showing everything. Chest hanging out; leaving nothing to the imagination. Why do men need to imagine what this woman really is like when you show everything in the street? Why would he want to marry you after you slept with him on the first date? He's thinking, "Man, who did she slept with *last* week on the first date?" All he had to do was buy you a cheap dinner, take you out for a drink and now you're opening your legs to allow him into you. You're so poisonous; you are a disease—because all he had to do was buy you a cheap dinner, and a drink. He's like, "Put this condom on, get my quick fix and it's over with." Now a week you're like, "He didn't call me back. I don't know why. No sweetheart! He had a good time!

You were a hooker. Not the kind that sold herself on the street, but you sold yourself for a quick meal and drink. You got a dinner;

he got some pootie tang. There is nothing else but the truth. If you want to be used and abused, you're making that choice. You let yourself be dictated and you never worked on the project of who you are and it all came full circle in the end.

Stop! Look at yourself and the life you want; you have to become that life. If you don't, you will keep getting the same treatment, and you will be alone. You will always be someone's mistress or a "Wham, bam thank-you" girl and never anyone's wife.

CHAPTER 6
ABUSE

Why do you believe you need to be abused? Maybe your parents or parent spanked you, maybe your grandparents spanked you, or someone hurt, abused, or attacked you. Whatever the circumstance, the question arises, "Why do we stay in abusive relationships?"

We stay because we feel we have no ways of leaving. Similar to the wives of military men, everything is in their husband's name. You can't do anything without your husband's permission; you feel alone and away from your support system. You choose to stay in an abusive relationship because of a house, this is my children's daddy or my children's mother." Is it because we feel we have nowhere to go despite the availability of shelters for battered spouses? If you have to go to a shelter, you go. You don't let anyone beat on you or take your life away, destroy your self-esteem or maybe even kill you. Why do we stay so long? Are we afraid of failure or what people are going to say or what people will think? As you close door and smile on the outside, the inside is hurting and you're crying every night.

You know there is a choice, and once again, the word "choice" comes up. Stop letting someone beat on you. Stop allowing someone to beat you up physically, emotionally and spiritually. You look like this, you look like that. Please walk away from that person. The first time a man place his hand on you the wrong way is the first time you should have walked away from that man.

The first time the man says something nasty to you, you should have walked away from that man. You are worth more than that. You are important. You are uniquely designed and made by God. You don't need anyone to beat on you. If it wasn't your mother or father, they don't need to put their hands on you.

You need to realize that you are worth something. You need to look in the mirror and say, "I am better than this. I am okay." I may not have everything that is needed or wanted in this season, however you will not abuse me. Open the door and walk out.

If you have to go to the shelter, home to your parents or parent, grandmother, aunt, uncle, best friend then you need to leave for safety and get help. You need to talk about it with someone you trust.

You need to work it out. You need to set a goal on staying out. Go to counseling; go to family that can help guide you in the right direction. Go to anyone that can give you the wisdom that you need to help make you stronger. You need to stop surrounding yourself with other negative people who say, "Oh, he really didn't mean it." Bull junk! Those people mean you no good. Anyone telling you to go back to being abused emotionally, physically, or spiritually does not mean you any good. You need to walk away from all of that negative environment. You need to move forward and say, "I am better than that. I am worth something." Look in the mirror every day and say, "I am worth something." The tears are coming down your eyes. "I am worth something. I am God's child. I am divinely made. I am important. I do not deserve to be treated that way." Until you believe in what you're saying, you may have to say it every day, but until you believe it with your whole being, you continue saying it. Look in that mirror, and eventually you will see the truth that you speak: that you are worth more than you been told and that you are designed to be your unique self. You do not have to take any kind of abuse from anyone, you have a choice.

You may convince yourself to stay and not walk away, but you need to choose to move forward for your betterment and safety. You need to walk away. You need to choose to believe in you and that you deserve better. Work on the project that is you and choose to dictate your life's direction.

CHAPTER 7

ILLNESS

This was a great topic because this was a deep topic for me. Illness. Overcoming sickness, disease, cancer, heart attacks, strokes, muscular syndrome, high blood pressure, cholesterol. Whatever your illness is, you can overcome it. You have to choose to overcome this illness by following your doctor's orders, eating right, and engaging in some physical exercise. You can learn to still live life and not exist with learning how to manage your illness.

When we sit there and allow this illness to become our identity, we expect and begin looking for pity parties. No! Illness is something that may have come upon you naturally and by means that are completely out of your control. So don't take fault in a situation that you have no power over. Sometimes illness comes because of the way we are treating our bodies. We're overweight, eating the wrong types of foods, not working out, and in some cases eating what we shouldn't because we're depressed and unhappy.

Gluttony is a sin; it's in the Bible. You are weighting two, three, even as much as four hundred pounds because you're choosing to not get up and make changes in our lives. You aren't taking any action to improve your health, so now you have high blood pressure, cholesterol problems, and diabetes; illnesses that are reversible if you make the choice to make changes. Let me get that Ben & Jerry's, let me get that piece of cake, that Krystals, Popeyes, KFC, or the pizza. You don't chose to work out, go walking, running, or incorporate healthy foods such as fruits, vegetables, nuts, or any other healthy choices. You're just going to get things that you know you shouldn't have because you want to cry and have a pity party; and that's your excuse to keep eating instead of saying, 'To heck with all that!" You need to look at yourself and say, "This is what it is going to be. I'm going to eat that apple, orange, or make a smoothie. I'm going to make better choices because I want to be better and live better!"

To help with these better choices, look at what you buy to put in your refrigerator. You have to start in the supermarket and not buy those unhealthy foods that serve no real purpose but to put you in an early grave. If you don't have it in your house, you will not have the choice to eat it. It's that simple. Stop buying it in the first place. You're wasting money purchasing all the bad food and you're preparing yourself for failure. I get it. It's your comfort food. Almost everyone likes and had their go-to comfort foods. Back in the day, it was macaroni and cheese, collard greens, gravy, rice, apple pie, or a piece of chocolate cake. We grew up on that comfort food, but we don't have to keep living with that comfort food everyday. These foods can be for special occasions; maybe on a Sunday. It's ok to treat yourself; but from Monday to Saturday, choose to eat with wisdom and discernment because you made the choice to live a longer healthier life.

Ladies, some of you like to describe that dream guy as this six foot two, around one hundred and eighty pound stud as your ideal partner. He looks like Denzel Washington or Thomas Rhett and makes plenty of money. I hear you ladies, but let's get real here. You definite know what type a man that you looking to obtain in your life. Who said he wants a three hundred pound woman? Don't get me wrong, ladies. It's not because of your weight; it's because of your health! No man wants to take care of a sickly woman. Stop complaining, and do something about it. Start walking fifteen minutes until you get to thirty minutes; do that thirty minutes three times a week. Cut back on what you eat. Get yourself to 1500 calories a day. Stop playing! You ask me; you got it. I'm not going to lie to you. I'm a straight forward person. I would love to cheat and eat all those calories and fat, but then I get on a scale and it makes me get up and start walking. I don't like doing exercise, but it is a way of life if I want to maintain my health and weight.. You come to me and say, "I want to meet somebody." You don't want to meet just anyone with a good heart that's going love you. You want the 6'2, healthy stud. He could be 5'0, love you with all his heart, and provide you with the best life, but you'll come up with some type of excuse as to why you don't want him. He's too skinny. He's too big or small. He doesn't meet your desires. You have to keep in mind your wants and needs are two different things.

Look! If you're over twenty-five, most likely, you are at the stage in your life or coming into the stage in your life where you want someone who is going somewhere; someone who has something going in their lives that you can build a life with. If you're over forty, you want somebody who is financially settled in his or her life. If you're over fifty, you want someone who has at least ten years on the job, with a house and car of their own, who is taking care of their responsibilies. If that person has child support, they're taking care of that and paying what is owed. If the person doesn't, walk away. If that person doesn't take care of their own blood, they're not going to take care you and yours. Be real, ladies, and stop playing around. You are always saying what you want, but what you need is different. You need someone who is going to love you, support you, and embrace you. You want to be embraced; that's the whole key to being there when you're sick and when you're not feeling well. When your job gets on your nerves, he wants to listen to you and hold your hand, and he's not ashamed of you.

You don't want anyone who doesn't touch you in public or who walks ahead of you. Are you crazy? That man doesn't love you if he doen't want to walk next to you or hold your hand; who is looking all around instead of being focused on you. You're three hundred pounds because you're paying all the bills, taking care of him, dressing him, doing his resume, getting him a new job, and helping him start a new life. Ladies, all you're doing is setting him up for the next woman. Are you crazy? Wake up!

Let's smell the coffee. I keep telling you that. You need to stop trying to dress someone up like a Barbie or Ken doll. Then he goes and gets a Barbie because he doesn't want you. You know what you're doing, but you continue to do this to hold on to him.

Ladies; love yourself as much as you love these men. Look in the mirror. Look in those eyes. Work on your project. Stop letting people dictate you. Start walking your walk and talking your talk and believing in it. A man likes a positive woman. Men like a woman who has good news and happy thoughts because they don't want to hear a woman complaining all the time; I don't want to hear a man complaining all the time. You need to look out for yourself, think for yourself, and move forward within yourself. We're choosing to let our illness control us.

CHAPTER 8

FINANCIAL PLANNING

Financial planning is a subject we don't like to talk about. As long as we get a pay check, we spend it; that's your financial plan. Nothing for the future. Nothing about life insurance. Nothing about making sure your children's college is ready to be paid for. Nothing that we do is financial planning.

Usually when you receive your pay check, we pay the rent or mortgage, gas bill, electricity bill, car note, household bills, gas to travel to and from work, food for the house, and something for the children and before you know it, you're broke. This shouldn't become your financial plan.

Uncle Sam takes his money out first. Taxes. Why don't we take our 10 percent out first and put that in savings, money markets, mutual funds, or IRAs, and start investing in our future? We don't do that because we were not taught to pay ourselves. We give our 10 percent to the church, but we still don't give our 10 percent to ourselves. We need to do financial planning. We need to use wisdom in our financial situations. We need to know how to budget our funds.

You may decide to have children one day or already have them and your child may desire to go to college and if you do not have a college fund set up, you are setting your child or children up for a life of debt from student loans. Those expensive clothes you bought could have been a different decision. You could have purchased something less expensive and deposited the money in a college fund or take twenty-five dollars a month and place it into a savings account for a rainy day. Make a plan; make a budget. You have an idea that you will be going to the movies, visiting friends and taking the children out to dinner. Do your budget; use wisdom. If you know you can't do it, that means you shouldn't go. Parks are free. Go to the park. There are a lot of free things in your area.

Start Googling events that are free for family or for singles. Go to them. Why not? Get out the neighborhood explore a little bit. Enjoy life. That's how you start living and stop existing. We are existing because of our financial planning; that is the real the truth. We're trying to live large.

We're trying to live a caviar life with a tuna-fish salary. Your salary is only tuna fish. Cut it out. You do not need to impress anyone. It's just like these Atlanta housewives; some of them were in foreclosure or in debt and we sit there like, "Oh yeah! She is going to the club. She's going here," she's getting into and driving that." And they're doing all of this for what? For somebody to see you? That's why you still can't pay your rent the next month. You have borrow from Paul to pay Peter and pay Peter to pay Paul. That is not living and if you're choosing that way of life you are not doing financial planning. Plan your budget, plan your life, and stick to it.

If you know you can't control your spending start putting your money in a saving account. Choose to have it taken out of your check and direct-deposit it into the savings account. Don't get an ATM card or online transfer to the account. Go back to the old way of using cash. You take out a certain amount of cash a month, and when the cash runs out, THAT'S IT; you're broke. You've used all the cash you can get for that month. Sit home, get a movie, watch TV, or read. Reading is beneficial to your mind. It seems everybody is glued to his or her Ipad, Iphone, Google, or whatever we have in this day and age and it's rare to see some old-fashioned book reading. Go to the library, Books are free. You don't have to buy them.

Do something constructive so your children can see you sitting down reading. Maybe they will sit down and follow your example. Everything is not video, TV, and computers. That is our time—yes it is—but it doesn't have to be our choice. We make that choice with our financial decisions, our examples, our planning. Again, work on your financial plan. This a part of your project that we spoke about earlier. You have to make another temporary choice and choose to live somewhere else or with someone else. This is called sacrifice. Sometimes we have to sacrifice to reach certain goals we have in life. You're making the choice. Don't complain to anybody and stop borrowing from everybody. People see you coming and they want to walk away because they know you're coming to ask for something. Stop having your hand out. Start living your life and start being independent. You have to kick the habit of depending on others. Educate yourself in how to become financially responsible and start planning to live life and stop existing.

CHAPTER 9

RELIGION

Religion is a word that people associate with being holier than thou. Now I understand some people are going to argue about this, but I don't believe in religion. I believe in God. I believe we all come from being created and we, as women sometimes, get so hung up in our church and religion: Pentecostal, AME, Baptist, CME, Methodist, Seventh-day Adventist, Jewish, Muslim, Catholic and Jehovah Witness whatever. It's great to believe.

I believe in God; that's my choice, but you may believe in a higher power that is called by another name. I am not here to judge anyone because my walk is to love all people. I believe all people are created equal, and I believe we all have a choice to move forward; we have a choice to love or not love as long as you can live with your choice. Some people think they belong in church four or five times a week and I'm not judging those people. However, if your children see you for five minutes, and you only have dinner in the microwave, and you're rushing out to worship service just because the doors are open and you are the usher. I have a personal problems with that.

A good leader should say, "Go home and be with your husband and your family," and say, "we have it today, sister so-and-so or brother so-and-so." You don't have to run every time the church doors are open. If you believe that you're the only person to complete the task, then there are some issues. You are really running away from your home, this is my personal opinion something is not right with that; and while you're praising and crying out to God just trying to make it right, you could try to go home and talk to your spouse to try and fix things. A good leader, male or female, who is guiding and who God calls to serve over others needs to notice his or her leadership team and congregation.

If you're leading a group of people and you notice there are many divorces in your congregation, that means something is wrong. That means you're talking preaching and teaching, but you're not being heard. I know some people may not agree with me, but as I stated previously, this is my personal opinion. The truth is *my* truth.

I was raised in church all my life. I have visited churches, chapels, temples, halls, for many years. There is nothing I haven't seen pertains to church and church culture and there is nothing wrong with it. We need a place to go for fellowship with someone of the same faith. That's a good thing. However, sometimes it can take over your life. Nothing should take over your life to a point that you aren't living. For example, you are unable to go on vacation because the church is having the women's retreat this week and this is the only week your husband and you both off from work. The clear choice should be you going with your husband. You dont' *have* to be at the women's retreat. We have to make choices for our relationship and our family. Second example the church is feeding the hungry, and I have to be there every fourth Sunday, but my daughter has a play. You don't go to church; you go with your daughter. You only have one time for her to do this play. The church can get somebody else to fill in your position. You think you are so indispensable. No one is indispensable.

Because you want that pat on the back or those bragging rights because you feel that pat on the back from brother or sister so-and-so is oh so important from the church leadership. It shouldn't be. My personal opinion is that I like to teach, preach and educate others with God's word, but I also like to sit in the back and talk to the members and get to know them and see what is really going on in their lives.

People die in the church. We have the funeral and everybody is crying. Brother or sister so-and-so is going to the funeral and we call him or her during the month of the service. Three to six months later, when that person really needs someone to call, do you call; even if they're a faithful member and you're doing the "church thing," do you check on them? No! You're busy doing your church thing. Another example would be if someone came up to you and said, "I'm getting married," and you go to conduct the premarital counsel. After the session you notice they do not need to be together, but they are faithful tithers, you're afraid to tell them, "No, do not marry this person," because you don't want to lose their money or respect.

I think we need to go back and do a little research on shepherding, but that is just my opinion. I love people who love people. Who really cares and who has time. You get so big you don't have time to talk to someone. Everyone has to make an appointment to see you, but I understand it the only way thing can get done in a timely matter. Maybe if the time was invested with qualify people teaching your leaders and not family or friends who may not be qualify in the subject area that being taught Some leaders are always leaving their wives and children at home and this can become very stressful. You may be looking at this example and may decide it is all right to be away from your spouse and children and your spouse should not complain. Their wives are always home with the children and they are always on the road speaking here and traveling there trying to get to that image because they want to be the next mega church or massive religion. They feel God called them, but God also gave them a duty as husband and wife and nothing comes between what God has put together. Do you remember that verse? However let's be fair. This may be their only income and they may have to travel and that's understandable; but if they are seeking more materialistic things rather than serving God, that's something to consider.

Now let's say you're a faithful ten percent tither, for an example; but your rent isn't paid. Your faith is that God will make a way; God gave us wisdom and discernment. Pay your rent, or you will be homeless. When you have no place to go, the church might help you out two or three times, and then they'll say, "Well, we can't help you out anymore with this." Now you're angry at the choice; however, you had a choice. It's not anyone fault but your own. Now you have to ask your family, "Oh, what did you do with your money?" You say, "Well, I gave it to the church," and your family is on your back. Well, they need to be on your back. Somebody needs to wake you up. What has happened is, you started living above your means. Yes, you should give, but give what you can financially afford or give it in time or talent, and if they don't appreciate that, then you might need to look for another place to worship.

I believe that my tithes are hopefully helping someone who is without. Someone who is homeless. Someone who needs a light bill paid. Someone who lost his or her job. Someone who just had a big medical expense. Not paying for a parking lot. I'm sorry. People are not going to like this, but I'm going to say what it is. Hey, it's life. Now, I believe the church is blessed in funds, and if they have the extra to do that, then that is fine. Taking care of the members, non-members and their community. We may need to think about our leadership and how it can be corrected to reflect a positive outcome.

We need to look at things and stop following just because we've been going to a church for five, ten, fifteen, twenty years and using that as an excuse to just stay. We need to grow. Leaders are supposed to grow and move people forward to serve. God said to edify, to teach, so they can go out and do their own. The fact that they're keeping members for thirty years; preaching the same message over and over, they are not doing what the word says as leaders, to me. Ladies, look at your place of worship, look at your life, and make your choices for you and not for what someone else thinks or expects you to do. That's what religion is. Stop just following and actually choose a faith that truly nurtures your spiritual and life direction.

CHAPTER 10

COMMITMENT

Commitment is not being committed to someone that doesn't want to be committed back to you. Commitment is not a one-sided deal. When you are committed to something, that means you are giving it your all in all. Point blank. When you are committed to your job, you need to give your best. I don't care if you don't like your supervisor. Thank God you have employment. Too many people don't have employment this day and time. Until another door opens, you stay your butt there. Don't be trying to get yourself fired. Don't bring yourself down to the person's level that you don't want to become. Start being committed to your employer, give it your best shot, and then, you maybe, you will be rewarded another position or promotion. Why should God reward us with the big things if we don't even want to take care of the little things?

If you have children, you need to have a commitment to them. They did not ask to be born. They did not ask to come out here. You opened your legs to enjoy the entertainment, and you gave birth to your child. Okay! You need to raise them. You need to put your husband and children after God and yourself and be committed to what they are doing to make them the best person they can be. That is your commitment. If you are single, you need to be committed to your household. Make sure that your children and you have a safe place to live. You travel to work, you come home, and you make sure your children have a safe place to go after school; that's your job. That's a commitment. If you are married, you have a commitment to your spouse. I know some people won't be happy with me for saying this, but if you cannot be committed to them, then it is time to move on because you are living a lie and no good comes out of that. I have seen some wonderful fifty-plus-year marriages. They were committed to each other to have a life time of happiness, growth, and raising their children.

In some cases, some people are designed to be together and are truly in love. In others cases, they stayed for the raising of the children. I have also had the experience of seeing couple whom divorce after twenty-five years of marriage or after the children graduate college and became bitter toward each other and life. There are instances where one could not afford to leave and felt empty inside because of the choices they made of not building a career for themselves and feeling like they would not survive on their own.

However, you also need to be truthful about the reason you are getting married. Do not get married because of financial reasons, children, emptiness, pregnancy, or friendship; only get married because you believe in that person and you want a life long commitment with them. Anything less than that will bring unhappiness, resentment, pain, and a life of hardship. I'm not pushing divorce, but I personally believe if you made a choice to please others, to help out a friend, to deal with a pregnancy, to run away from something, to adhere to your belief system, to grow your career, or any other reason besides love, it will not work out for your happiness. Remember, you and only you are the one that has to live with your choices; everyone has an opinion of what someone else should do. My personal opinion is to make the right choice for you, and if you have children, your children have to have a healthy life to live and not exist.

CHAPTER 11

EASY ACCESS

You decide to sleep around with everybody, and then ask yourself, "Why you can't find Mr. Right." Maybe because you have easy access; in other words, opening your legs to every, Paul, Theodore, Evans, or Peter. Most men do not want used baggage that has slept all over the place.

On the first date, most men are looking and watching, to see if you will offer sex on the first date. Most likely if they enjoyed the sex, they may tap that and date you for another three months but will never marry you.

You chose to open your legs to them and in the back of their minds, they are asking, "I wonder who else has she slept with on the first night?"

If you become easy access to every man you meet, maybe you need to put marriage out of the picture because you will always be the one that they will not bring home to Mother. You will have to change your life style and look inside to see what is going on and why you feel that you have to be easy access to every man that gives you a little attention. Your body is your temple and you should protect and guide it from anything and anyone that will not respect and love you.

On the flip side, with all the sexually transmitted diseases out here, you need to see why you do not value your life enough. It is time to take the mirror out and see what is going on inside or get some counseling to help you understand your behavior. Then "maybe" you can get yourself together because you can have a true committed relationship with someone else.

Stop sleeping around. Every time you sleep with someone, you lose a little piece of yourself to that person and when the right person, finally, comes around, you can't even tell because your heart is gone. You've opened your legs to countless number of men and now you are empty inside. You, then, start lusting, fornication, whoring around, or whatever you want to call it and, in the end, you are the one who has to judge where your life has gone and live it. You're making the choices in your life. Get to the point where you feel you can turn your life around. It's never too late to change. Ladies stop giving it away. Stop being easy access and learn to love yourself by living and stop existing. Simple, plain English; if you are not ready for a commitment, stop playing games.

Stop saying there are no good men around any more. Yes, there are good men! Maybe they have been used, abused, hurt and are shying away. When you are blessed with a good one, you don't even know it because you did not give yourself time to recoup from the bad relationship. Most men do not recover as fast as women after being hurt. They're scared of commitment after what someone else did. Now they say, "Wait on me. Give me time.

Let me treat you right," when he is just seeing you in a one-on-one relationship. He is not sleeping in your bed. He is not shacking up with you. You have a committed relationship. You can visit his house and he can visit your house without worrying about someone else being over there. You both should be moving forward toward the next step working to build a relationship with a common goal. If not, then you let it be what it's going to be. Don't blame anyone else because the choice is yours. You chose to be uncommitted. A true, lasting relationship will require you to commit and usually doesn't settle for anything else.

CHAPTER 12

COMMON SENSE

Do we have or do we use our common sense? Most of us do not. Capital N-O-T. We have common sense that is in us, but we choose not to use it. What I mean is that it will make us see the truth in things. It doesn't take a book or a doctorate degree to make us see things in life. For whatever reason, there are times where we seems to ignore our common sense. It may be that we are afraid of something. Perhaps we are unsure of an outcome of a situation or, maybe, we just don't want to know the outcome of it. It may be an instance where we don't want people to know our secrets. Common sense is our everyday inner voice that we rely on to make wise decisions throughtout our daily lives.

For example: we meet a man. The man has a nice smile, has a nice car, and talks a great game. We believe everything he said, and you don't know it, but our common sense is telling us to slow down. We move forward. We go running to him. He states he lives in a place you've never been and he never takes you to his house. Every time we're meeting up, it's always in a restaurant and we're never going to popular places. Our common sense is saying he might be married or have a girlfriend; but, for some reason, we're choosing to ignore that common sense. When he comes over, it is always after twelve o'clock at night or at five o'clock in the morning. He's never available on Saturadays or Sundays; only Monday through Friday. It seems we, only, always travel to places way out of town and never places right around the neighborhood.

Common sense is telling you something is not right and we choose not to pay attention. Then one day, common sense is looking you straight in the face. Here comes his wife. "You're with my husband? You're calling my husband? We have three children." Common sense warned us, but we chose not to listen to it. Then, after knowing the truth, we keep sneaking and hiding with this man. Why is that? Is it because we are so scared of being alone that we don't want the empty bed even though it is empty the majority of the time because he is with his wife: or do we not have any respect. We are choosing not to use our common sense.

When we are on a job, common sense tells us not to tell a person our personal business. Common sense tells us, "Don't share," but we share. We don't realize this person has been on the job before us, and they already have friends. You share your secrets, then she share your secrets with another person, and, now, the whole office knows your business. Now you're angry and want to quit the job because everybody knows your business, but your common sense told you not to share, but you decided to share.

Another example is your husband coming home late. Your husband's hours change all of a sudden. He has to go on the road on an overnight trip. Your husband smells like perfume. Your husband doesn't want to have sex cause he's tired. Common sense is telling you something is wrong, but you tell yourself, "No, he's just tired. He's paying the bills, right? Common sense tell you to be aware. In the meantime, what are you doing? The same thing. Not making any preparations. Not looking out for anyone; including you and your children. What are you doing? Nothing. Common sense told you. He comes in three months later: "I want a divorce." He's got another woman and he wants to take care of her children. He's happier, and he moved all the accounts. You can't find any money. You can't find anything because he handles everything; you never got involved in the family business or the financial planning of the household even thought your common sense told you to. You're left alone with nothing. You may have child support as long as he working and do not quit his job. Your common sense told you to prepare. Why did't you listen to your common sense?

Now you're alone. You have to find a job and take care of the children. You're too proud to call Mommy and Daddy so you call a friend. You tell her what happened and she tells somebody else. Now everyone knows your business. You're too embarrassed and now you're not talking to anybody because you're angry with everybody, but it was you who didn't use your God-given common sense.

Common sense: does it help us or does it hurt us when used in the different aspects of our lives? Do you live or are you existing? That's common sense.

CHAPTER 13

DREAMERS

Dreamers are people who dream of everything in their lives. They dream of their future. They have it preplanned. "I'm going to get married. I'm going to have six bridesmaids, six grooms-men, a ring boy and flower girl." "I'm going to buy a house on the rich side of town. I want to get a promotion at my job."

The dreamers. No plan, just dreams. Year after year, the dreams don't come true; we get discouraged. Instead of making a new plan, we stick to the dream. You find somebody to marry you and your dreams, not even knowing what his dreams are. You marry him, and you think you are going to be happy; you don't even know him, but he fits the dream. You get with him, he doesn't clean up, and he doesn't pick up. He doesn't even talk. No communication. You go and get pregnant; that's the dream: two children. You have two children knowing something is not right. You never took care of the project of yourself. Never using common sense. Never doing anything to prepare. However you kept that dream alive, and nothing is going to stop this dream. You have purchased your dream home, which added more debt that you cannot afford. Now, you dream husband get laid off from his job and you're fussing and cussing all of the time at him. You think to yourself, "It's his fault. He needs to get a second job and do better. He needs to make more money. He needs to talk to you and he needs to help you. "Why should he? You took care of him. You were the one that had the dream. You already had the foundation and the perfect picture. You just threw him in as a landmark. It wasn't both of your dreams; it was YOUR dream. Your house is about is about to be foreclosed, your car is about to be repossessed, and your children can't go to private school. You have no money to do anything.

The dreamer. It was your dream. It was not his fault, but you went and told your friends he's no good, he's not being a man. A man gets tired of being told that he is no good by his woman. Then he starts acting out and actually being no good. He then walks out of the door. Now, where are your dreams? You never knew if you really had a good man or not because you were too focused on your own goals and your own dreams. That's the dreamer. Dreamers need to look in the mirror at themselves before following their dreams.

CHAPTER 14

MOTIVATION

Motivation is something that we do to try to help others reach another level in their lives. But how do we motivate ourselves? What do we do to motivate? Do we make a goal? Have a plan? Do you have a direction? Or do we just say we're motivating ourselves? Most of us are motivated by something we heard, something we read or something we did. Sometimes it is hard to motivate oneself. Self-motivation is the toughest thing for some people because it causes us to look at ourselves while we are not being motivated.

Motivation is a thing of desire. It's a thing of reaching a new direction; it's a thing of walking another path on our journey in this life. Motivation is not saying, "I'm going to do" or "I can't do." These statement are not motivation. Motivation is "I will reach this goal" or "I can achieve these things," "I can find my direction," and "I will accomplish it." That's talking motivation.

Staying around you and you are negative is not motivating and can create a lonely life. No one likes to be around someone that is always negative. Never happy, always complaining. If that is you, it's time for a new motivation. The motivation should be "I can," "I will," and "I have." That's motivation. Surround yourself with positive people. Positive things, positive goals, positive directions. Do not just stay negative. If you want to be negative, then you need to be with other negative people and existing in life.

A motivating person is encouraging. We need not take everything personally; we need not take everything negatively. When someone is trying to motivate and help you to reach a direction in your life, then you should listen and accept that they may know a little something about where you are going and how to make the changes that you need. However, the choices is yours. It's not your mother, father, husband, or your children that stop you from getting somewhere.

You have to be self-motivated. You have to be your own motivation. You also have to use the things that encourage you. If you want to be motivated, then you have to surround yourself with positivity. Read positive books, listen to positive people, and listen to positive music. Stop putting things in the air that are negative; stop reading things that are negative.

The steps toward motivation is stop complaining and start doing and become motivated; the only one stopping you once again is you. Look in the mirror and see who your motivation is. It's you that can motivate you. Surround yourself with positive people and do positive things in your life. If that does work, the only one to blame is you. Start living and stop existing. Motivate yourself to live.

CHAPTER 15

CHEATER

Woman to woman, let's sit down and talk. We all have been cheated on or been the one that has done the cheating. Let's be honest; let's be for real. Woman to woman, when your man is out there with another woman, why do you want to go fight her? Why do you want to attack her? Why do you want to blame her? She had nothing to do with your relationship with your man. Your man made that commitment to you; you made that commitment to him. But you want to go and fight the other woman—for what reason? She didn't do anything to you; she's a woman, and she went after what she wanted.

"Yeah, she knew he was married. Yeah, she knew you were in a relationship." She knew he was fine; he was out there. Where were you? He was out there, met her at work, met her at the bar, met her at the club, met her in church, met her in the grocery store, in the post office, or wherever he met her. He was the one who made the commitment to you. He was the one who was supposed to be faithful to you. He was the one that betrayed you, so why do you want to fight the other woman? For real? What did she do? She just went after the fine man that came in the store, just like you thought he was fine, and he had a line, and she fell for it, and she didn't care about that ring. She went after what she wanted; you went after him. You looked at him and said, "He's going to be my husband. That's going to be my man." But you want to get angry when somebody else did the same things. Well, the thing is, what were you doing? How was he being treated at home? Were you nagging him? Were you telling him everything you're not going to do? Were you holding back on the sex? Were you not cooking? Did you want to care for him? Did you listen to him emotionally? Did you watch any sports with him? Did you want to spend any time with him? What were you doing? What made him go out there to get that other woman?

If you want to blame her, maybe you need to look in that mirror one more time. Maybe you weren't there, or you really weren't a good wife. Maybe you were cooking, cleaning, and taking care of the children and you're too tired, and he comes home and you have a t-shirt on, and your hair wasn't done. Your face looking like who-did-it-and-ran? When you were trying to get him to marry you, everything was looking good. You made sure you had makeup on, your hair pushed back and everything was in the right place. You did everything to get his attention but once you had him, what happened? You figure you have him now so you can stop trying to look good. You are the one who decided to gain the extra 50 pounds and told him the things you weren't not going to do anymore. He started looking around and someone else decided they wanted him, gave him some attention. They told him how nice he was and how fine he was looking. Yeah, you know some men are weak. Yeah, they are weak and they don't think with the right head sometimes. You know that. You knew what type of man he was when you met him. Who was he dating when you met him? Who was he married to when you met him? Why did he get divorced if he wasn't married anymore? You tell me? You know you want to complain, but you want to go fight another woman for this man. Please. Let the man go. If he doesn't want you, you don't need him. Why do you think you need to hold on to something just because you sat there and had two, three, or four children with him? You are the one who opened your legs and decided to have those babies. Maybe the first child was planned but the others could have been planned or not, because birth control is plentiful these days. However, all children are a blessing.

He couldn't have created those babies without you; you know what birth control is; you should have used it. If you did not want more children, you shouldn't have had them. You need to be willing to love them and keep them no matter if that man is there or not. Give those children the best life you can and file for child support. He may have left you, he can't run from his responsibilities.

Stop blaming the other woman because she went after your man. Your man was the one who broke the commitment. You need to talk to him, not her, and if he doesn't want to respect you and stay and work it out or go through counseling, then you need to let him go. Stop trying to hold on to someone that doesn't want to stay with you. My mother always said, "If it is for you, it will come back to you." It is up to you to choose your destination in life. It is your choice to keep him, let him go, or to forgive him." You know things are not what you want them to be. Let's get real now. You want to blame the other woman because she was out there looking good and smelling good. What are you doing about youself? Yeah, you take care of the children, but you can still look good doing it. I'm not saying you need to look like movie star every time you go out of the door, but make sure your hair is in place and your face is clean, your breath is smells good.

Whatever the situation may be, you should always keep yourself together; not for him but for yourself. Ladies, just because you have children doesn't mean that you have to stop being a beautiful woman. Put a little lip gloss or lipstick on those lips. You're tired, you have a rag on your head or you did not brush your hair today, you slapped on a wig that doesn't even look good on you, but you want to know why your man is looking in another direction? All right. Be real, and look in the mirror. Stop all the lies and jokes and get serious with yourself. If you want to blame someobody, then blame yourself. In order to keep your man, then the same way you got him should be the same way you keep hime. Stop fighting the other woman and start living your life.

CHAPTER 16
WHY MEN WALK AWAY

Why do some men walk away? Why did he leave you? Maybe he wasn't happy, maybe he never loved you, maybe he never really wanted you, or maybe you chased him away. Let's evaluate this stance.

A man might walk away because he was never committed in the first place; he didn't even know what he really wanted. He didn't know that he really did not want to be in a committed relationship. He might have been in a relationship because that was what someone told him that he was supposed to do. Or, maybe you chased him away. Maybe you cursed him out, maybe you argued, maybe you're nagging, maybe you're complaining, maybe you really don't know, but because he walked away, your worth is still something.

Stop trying to go blame yourself as the reason to why he walked away. He might have had his own demons, his own reasons, his own irresponsibilities. He didn't want to pay the bills, he didn't want to be a dad. He didn't want to be a husband. Those are his problems; those are not yours. Stop taking on his problems because he walked away. He sought out another woman; and thought the grass would be greener on the other side, but that is still his problem. Women, stop picking up their problems as your own.

Let him go. Heck, he wants to go... Bye! See you tomorrow. Never again. Tell him to get lost. Thank you for the season. Shake it off, "give yourself 30 days". Cry about it; and get over it.

Thirty days is all you should waste on someone who did not want you. Because you are your own person. You get yourself back out there. Get yourself back in the game. Get yourself together. Get your finances together. Get your health and physical body in order. Take time to do for you and stop worrying about getting another man because this one walked away from you. Take the time to explore how you can become better for yourself. Stop allowing someone else to make you accountable for who you are. You become accountable for who you are; men walk away. They do it every day. The heck with them. You don't need them, move on ladies.

Look at yourself. If you're doing what you are supposed to do, then the right man will come in your life at the right time. Stop trying to make things happen. The energy you wasted on that man— put it in you and your children and get your life together. Stop blaming yourself for other people's decisions. Life is too short, and every season is a new season, so look at it. Celebrate that this season is over and done with. Let me move forward to the next season. Look in the mirror and say "**my life is worth something. I am someone. I am uniquely designed. God had made me and I am worth a new season and a new life and whomever is supposed to be for me is for me.**"

CHAPTER 17

WHAT IS LIVING?

Living is when you have a life that makes you really happy, deep down in your bones and your soul. Living is when you have chosen path that allows you to really live your life in peace and harmony. You came up with a plan, you had a direction, and you followed it. You took your journey, your good and your bad, and you made a life for yourself. You're living. You have your dreams, you are going on vacation, and you have time to enjoy your family and friends. You're living and working in a career field that you enjoy. You have the home that you want. You're living in the state where you want to be; you have good friends and family. You can breathe every night; you can wake up every morning with joy in your heart. You can go to bed and say, "Thank you for this day" that's what I consider living.

Living is when you are not worried about debts. You are not exhausted. You are not uncomfortable. You have directions and goals. You are happy when you achieve your goals. Living is when you can say, "I love my life," and truly mean it in your heart. I love the things I do. I love the choices that I made and I don't have to do the things I don't want to do. That's what I consider living.

Living is all those things that you enjoy. I believe living is every day I wake up and I have a jump in my step and I get out of bed and say, "Thank God for another day." I believe living is when I can say I'm taking a trip and I will be back when I feel like being back. My direction is the path that I made, and at this age, I consider my life living. I can do what I want. I can say what I want, but also I know how to love because I know who gave me the strength to do this, which is God in my life and whichever higher power that is in your life.

I thank God for teaching me how to live, and I hope this book teaches you how to live and to stop existing and let your life be a life that you could be proud of and you can enjoy. But this did not come overnight for me, and it will not come overnight for you. It took sadness, happiness, and a lot of tears. Things that happened in my life that could have destroyed me, but I made a choice to live. It took sickness, illness, abuse, divorce, marriage and divorce again. Do not let the negative things that have happened in your life people hurting you, mistreating you or people saying that you would never amount to anything-detour you from your happiness. You have a choice to become whoever or whatever you would like to be..

I'm still walking my journey. I don't believe my journey is over yet, but I believe you can start your journey if you have not started it and start making your own directions, your own goals, and you can have a life that you live and you can be happy like I am now. I thank God for everything he has done, and I hope you can say the same one day. Stop Existing and Start Living.

CHAPTER 18

EMBRACE

Embrace Support Ministries was designed in January 2006, and it was designed to help support the dreams and desires of women around the world. We inspire **women** by mentoring them and helping them to reach their full potential in life. We help them realize that their passion to succeed is truly designed and **can be accomplish** all that they set out to do in their lives.

Embrace teaches women to believe in themselves and that all women are designed to be fruitful. We have **opened** our door to young women in college to help them focus on a straight and narrow path in their future. We meet in small groups so we can be more intimate and more confidential.

This organization is also the backing for this book.

We are established in the physical, emotional, and spiritual part of a woman. We care about all three areas, and this book covered a lot of topics, but it is really just to wake you up and to let you know there are two things you have to face and deal with before you can go to the next level.

Your weight gain might not be just from your physical attributes. It might be emotional; it might be a spiritual loss in your life. Embrace is engaged in making you a full, healthy woman. Your size on a scale doesn't dictate who you are, but the emotion of who you feel you are is what helps design who you are. And your spiritual is something to give you a lift when you are by yourself in those lonely hours.

Embrace the questions "Are you living? Or are you existing?" Hopefully this will help you in achieving and developing the best you when dealing with any situation in your journey during each season of your lives. Plus it will help you be stronger women by empowering and inspiring you to succeed.

If you're interested in becoming a part of Embrace or learning how to start a branch of Embrace in your state or your country, please email us at embracesupport@gmail.com. For update information please see our website www.embracesupport.com and follow us on Facebook, LinkedIn and Twitter under Embrace Support Ministries 25% sales of this book will be donated to Embrace Support Ministries to help women and college students.

ACKNOWLEDGMENTS

To my loving sons
John Jomar Glover Jr., James Glover, and Craig Adams,
who have always loved, supported, and encouraged me to continue this
journey in life
To my granddaughters, who are my special gifts: this book one day will
help guide you
Shinayah Toodles-Glover, Essence Glover, and Angel DeSouza-Glover
To my mentors and inspirational leaders:
Mr. David A. Rutledge
Mr. Elliot King
Dr. Percy Johnson
Dr. Robert C. Connor Sr.
Dr. Kerwin B. Lee
Dr. Kevin Lee
In memory of all the mothers who empowered me to be the best woman
of God:
Late Anne B. Connor (You gave birth to me)
Late Victoria Shaw(You raise me)
Juanita Kelly (You love me)
Luvenia McCant (You gave me spiritual guidance)
Late Annie Mae Glover-Murchison, Late Vernell Carson, Late Dorothy
Faulk, Late Essie M. Beard, Late Mary Toon

__To all my chosen sisters who always had my back and never gave up__
__on me:__
Sandra M. Faulk (fifty-three years of friendship)
Cynthia Miller (twenty-six years of friendship)
Lynn Burn-Wilson (forty-four years of friendship)
Charlotte Benson (twenty years of friendship)
Velinda Bailey (twenty years of friendship)
Sharon LaVale (forty-three years of friendship)
Sharon Grant (twenty-nine years of friendship)
Late Donna Shaw-Dabney (cousin)
Jennifer Faulk (fifty years of friendship)
Christine Johnson (twenty-eight years of friendship)
Sharon Benbow (thirty-six years of friendship)

To my inspiration in writing, my niece:
Melinda Nelson-William

Thank you to my siblings for loving me:
Shirley Ford, Jean Connor, Cornelious Connor and Michelle Byrd

Thank you to all the Embrace board members, present and past, and committee members for your support:

Attorney Cynthia Miller
Dr. Percy Johnson
Dr. Albert Scott
Dr. Walter Faulkner
Mr. Elliot King
Mr. Jerry Wilson PA
Mr. Joseph Parks
Faith Smith (eight years of friendship)
Renee Robinson (eight years of friendship)
Linda Weatherby (five years of friendship)
Nalani Asha Brooks (eight years of friendship)
Tanisha Skipper (eight years of friendship)
Jackie Davis (cousin)

A special thank you for everyone of my adopted children and supporter of Embrace
A special thank you to my daugther in law Shanoa Toodles-Glover

A special thank you for Editing this book
Steven Morrison
Dana Bonds

Thank you to my typist:
Chasity Burton

EMBRACE ARE YOU LIVING? OR ARE YOU EXISTING?
USE THESE BLANK PAGES FOR YOUR PERSONAL NOTES;

HOW ARE YOU GOING TO START LIVING AND STOP EXISTING?

EMBRACE ARE YOU LIVING? OR ARE YOU EXISTING?
USE THESE BLANK PAGES FOR YOUR PERSONAL NOTES;

HOW ARE YOU GOING TO START LIVING AND STOP EXISTING?

EMBRACE ARE YOU LIVING? OR ARE YOU EXISTING?
USE THESE BLANK PAGES FOR YOUR PERSONAL NOTES;

HOW ARE YOU GOING TO START LIVING AND STOP EXISTING?

EMBRACE ARE YOU LIVING? OR ARE YOU EXISTING?
USE THESE BLANK PAGES FOR YOUR PERSONAL NOTES;

HOW ARE YOU GOING TO START LIVING AND STOP EXISTING?

EMBRACE ARE YOU LIVING? OR ARE YOU EXISTING?
USE THESE BLANK PAGES FOR YOUR PERSONAL NOTES;

HOW ARE YOU GOING TO START LIVING AND STOP EXISTING?

www.ingramcontent.com/pod-product-compliance
Lightning Source LLC
Chambersburg PA
CBHW070057100426
42740CB00013B/2864